Colors

Red

Nancy Harris

Heinemann Library
Chicago, Illinois

HEINEMANN-RAINTREE

TO ORDER:
☎ Call Customer Service (Toll-Free) **1-888-454-2279**
🖥 Visit **heinemannraintree.com** to browse our catalog and order online.

©2008 Heinemann-Raintree
an imprint of Capstone Global Library, LLC
Chicago, Illinois

Editorial: Rebecca Rissman
Design: Kimberly R. Miracle and Joanna Hinton-Malivoire
Photo Research: Tracy Cummins and Tracey Engel
Production: Duncan Gilbert

Originated by Dot
Printed and bound by South China Printing Company
The paper used to print this book comes from sustainable resources.

ISBN-13: 978-1-4329-1587-2 (hc)
ISBN-10: 1-4329-1587-8 (hc)
ISBN-13: 978-1-4329-1597-1 (pb)
ISBN-10: 1-4329-1597-5 (pb)

12 11
10 9 8 7 6 5 4 3

**Library of Congress
Cataloging-in-Publication Data**

Harris, Nancy, 1956-
  Red / Nancy Harris.
    p. cm. -- (Colors)
Includes bibliographical references and index.
ISBN 978-1-4329-1587-2 (hc) -- ISBN 978-1-4329-1597-1 (pb) 1.
Red--Juvenile literature. 2. Colors--Juvenile literature. I. Title.
  QC495.5.H3766 2008
  535.6--dc22
                    2008005971

Acknowledgments

The author and publisher are grateful to the following for permission to reproduce copyright material: ©Alamy **p. 19** (Kathy deWitt); ©age fotostock **p. 7** (Vstock); ©Corbis **pp. 14, 23a** (DLILLC); ©istockphoto **pp. 5** Bottom Middle (Ljiljana Jankovic), **5** Top Right (Reuben Schulz), **8** (David Hughes), **13** (Jeff Goldman); ©photos.com **pp. 5** Top Left, **11**; ©Shutterstock **pp. 4** Bottom Left (coko), **4** Bottom Middle (Maceofoto), **4** Bottom Right (Vova Pomortzeff), **4** Top Left, **10, 22a** (RexRover), **4** Top Right (emin kuliyev), **5** Bottom Left (fat_fa_tin), **5** Bottom Right, **5** Top Middle (Susan Gottberg), **6** (Kathryn Bell), **9** (Tito Wong), **12, 22b** (william wyrick), **15** (Lori Martin), **17** (Chris Fourie), **18** (Harvey Hessler), **21** (Halldor Eiriksson), **22c** (Ronald Sumners); ©SuperStock **pp. 4** Top Middle (Photographers Choice RF), **16** (Creatas), **20, 22d, 23b** (BlueMoon Stock).

Cover photograph reproduced with permission of ©Getty Images/ Duane Rieder.

Back cover photograph reproduced with permission of ©Corbis/ DLILLC.

The publishers would like to thank Nancy Harris for her assistance in the preparation of this book.

Every effort has been made to contact copyright holders of any material reproduced in this book. Any omissions will be rectified in subsequent printings if notice is given to the publisher.

Disclaimer

Contents

Red

Are all plants red?

Are all animals red?

Are all rocks red?

Are all soils red?

Plants

Some leaves are red.

Some leaves are not red.

Some stems are red.

Some stems are not red.

Some flowers are red.

Some flowers are not red.

Animals

Some feathers are red.

Some feathers are not red.

Some scales are red.

Some scales are not red.

Some fur is red.

Some fur is not red.

Rocks

Some rocks are red.

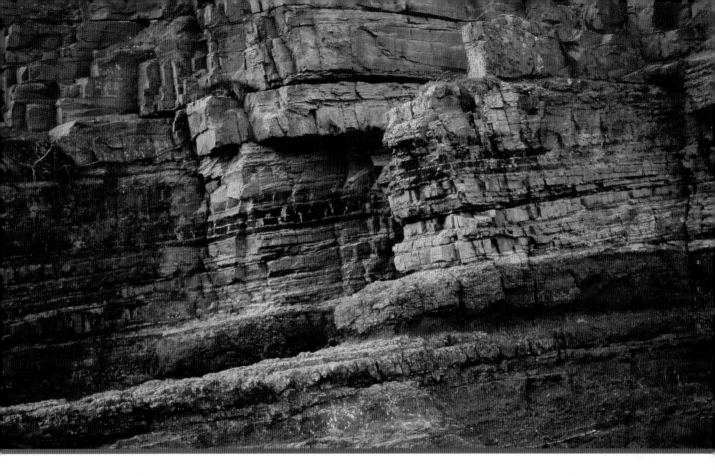

Some rocks are not red.

Soil

Some soil is red.

Some soil is not red.

What Have You Learned?

Some plants are red.

Some animals are red.

Some rocks are red.

Some soils are red.

Picture Glossary

 **scale** small plate that covers the body of some animals

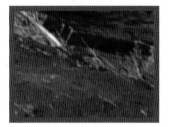 **soil** mix of small rocks and dead plants. Plants grow in soil.

Content Vocabulary for Teachers

body covering   outer layer, such as skin or scales, that protects an animal
color   depends on the light that an object reflects or absorbs

Index

Note to Parents and Teachers

Before reading:
Talk with children about colors. Explain that there are many different colors, and that each color has a name. Use a color wheel or other simple color chart to point to name each color. Then, ask children to make a list of the colors they can see. After they have completed their list, ask children to share their results.

After reading:
Ask children to think about different red objects. Then, help them to write acrostic poems for the word red. For example:

Raspberries

Erasers

Dresses